THIS BOOK BELONGS TO:

Silly Lily

& Her Feeding Tube

To my loving family,
who have always been my rock
and my biggest supporters,
thank you for your unwavering love
and encouragement.

To my amazing boyfriend,
who has stood by my side through thick and thin,
your love and strength have been my guiding light.

And to my best friend Carrigan,
who has faced her own health challenges
with unparalleled courage,
you are the epitome of inspiration, bravery,
and strength.

This book is dedicated to all of you,
for believing in me and being my pillars of strength.

Thank you for being my constants
in a world of uncertainties.

Hey! Have you met this girl named Lily?

She's fun and thoughtful and really rather silly!

She loves school and playing with her friends.
But when the lunch bell rings, all of that ends.

Lily gets sad when it's time to eat.
Whether it be breakfast, dinner,
or time for a treat.

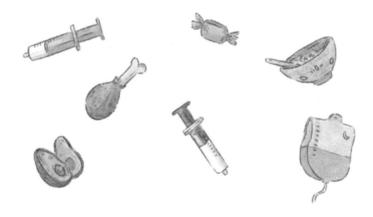

Lily feels left out
because of her feeding tube; you see.
It's a different way to eat, much different
than you and me.

Lily doesn't like feeling all alone.
She talked to her teacher, so she wasn't
on her own.

"Why am I different? Why is it so hard?"

Then her teacher reminded her

to let down her guard.

"It's okay to be different," Ms. Nasser says with a smile.

"Everyone is special, they just need to be reminded once in a while."

But Lily sure didn't feel special and wished she didn't have to eat like that.

150

She wished she could be more like her friends Bella, Steve, and Matt.

Ms. Nasser didn't like to see Lily feeling so down.

Especially when she's usually silly

and dancing around.

She decided to plan a very special outing
to boost Lily's mood.

And it started with Ms. Nasser
making Lily's favorite food.

She had planned a picnic with all of Lily's class.

It was set up outside of the school on the grass.

They blended all the food, so they didn't have to chew.

Just what Lily was used to,
and she couldn't believe it was true.

"You're all blending up your food!"

Lily says with a grin.

She finally feels happy to eat and like she fits in.

She even shows her friends how her feeding tube works.

They were interested and enthused,

and it made Lily smirk.

It was the first time that Lilly
didn't feel left out.
She wanted to jump up and down
and laugh and shout.

She thanked Ms. Nasser for helping her feel unique.

She no longer felt awkward, sad, or weak.

Lily says, feeling fine, beautiful, fun, and free.

Sometimes we just need a reminder
that it's okay to stand out.

A reminder to embrace your differences
and never feel doubt.

Because just like Lily – you are unique,
beautiful, and true.

And in this whole world,
there is no one else like you!

"I love being myself,"
Lily says in her own silly way.
Something she promises to remember,
each and every day!

"Go on! Embrace your differences and be sure to stand tall!"

Lily says, as she looks at you, "it's a lesson for all!"

Meet the Author!

Madison Holden's journey from aspiring teacher to the founder of the Silly Lily Foundation is a testament to resilience and determination. Despite facing multiple rare chronic illnesses that altered her career path and daily life, Madison found a creative outlet through creating the character of Silly Lily. Through Silly Lily, she strives to inspire children facing challenges by emphasizing the beauty and strength in their uniqueness.

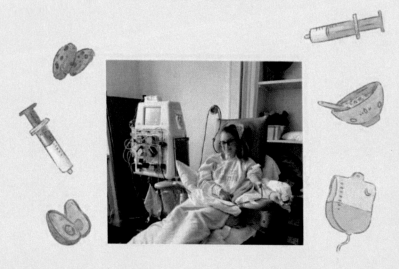

Meet the Illustrator!

From a very young age, Emily loved being creative, and growing up, she was lucky enough to connect with a wide variety of people from all walks of life, this made her fall in love with the casual magic of day to day life. She used to work in hospitality, filling up her sketchbooks on her days off, but one day she reached a catalyst and decided to give her illustration career a chance. She has since illustrated a wide range of children's books focusing on emotional well-being, using her watercolor illustrations to convey beautiful messages like this one.

Silly LILY
NON-PROFIT

The Silly Lily Foundation, a non-profit organization founded by Madison, not only sells books but also donates them to children, families, schools, and hospitals.

Through the support of generous sponsors, Silly Lily is able to bring smiles to the faces of children by providing them with books that reflect their own experiences.

The impact of seeing a character like Lily and feeling a sense of connection and representation is truly special and meaningful for those who receive these books.

Madison's dedication to turning her personal struggles into a source of comfort and empowerment for others showcases the transformative power of creativity, empathy, and generosity. Silly Lily stands as a beacon of hope for children in difficult circumstances, reminding them that they are not alone and that their uniqueness is a gift to be celebrated.

Through her foundation, Madison has created a lasting legacy of compassion and support for those in need.

With Love,
The Silly Lily Foundation

Made in United States
Orlando, FL
29 July 2024

49673415R00018